LUNAR

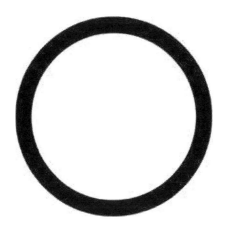

Lunar Tattoos by Will Vigar

Hastings Beach 1974, An Autopsy, Kiss Me Again Jack and A Deserted Village previously published by A Swift Exit's anthology 'Absent Ginsberg' and used with permission.

First Edition Published February 2018

ISBN: 9781980251293

Special thanks to Dave Kurley, Dave Hubble, Vanella Mead, Greg Gilbert, everyone at The Trago Lounge especially Reuben, Steve and John, and, of course, Andy Malinowski.

www.willvigar.net
despitedenseweed.wordpress.com
Please consider sponsorship through patreon.com/willvigar

Contents

A Deserted Village

An Architect would no doubt weep
at the maze of tumbled rock found
sad, lonely, lost beneath the sweep
of beaten bracken paths. Summer

brings bright silence with each new dawn.
The shadow of Hound Tor retreats
revealing a hamlet, not mourned,
resting in nature's verdant shroud.

Man forgotten, sheep and goats graze,
skylarks spar with zephyrs over
wild flowers, wild herbs, wildlife. A place
of plague, abandoned, lost in thyme.

Church Ope Cove

Tethered kelp shakes
angry algal fists
at boy racer waves

reaching for shore.
Slow-time tides beat
lunar tattoos.

Oil black mackerel
taunt the shore bound;
Slick and shifting.

Wind whips; lips chapped;
horse-tail salt slaps.
Breathe in brine.

Hastings Beach 1974

Ignoring the arguments and the cigarette fug,
I rub the condensation from the window.
It won't be long before white noise stops
its sibilant assault on roof and windscreen.

Rolling down the window, just a crack,
to breathe in fresh salt air with a sad veneer
of vinegar sharpness, wet chips, boiled whelks.
The weather-thwarted seaside treat plays out

as it always has.

I drown the sibling tantrums out; slot machines
are not that important. I'm content enough
to sip Heinz Tomato Soup from the plastic
top of a well-worn Thermos flask and lose myself

in the relentless beauty
of raging, murderous waves.

Davy's of Dover

Tottering on the stub and clack,
my Mum, replete in navy slacks,
ushers us to Davy's van
to buy us fish and chips.

The salt and fat and ketchup packs
The chips and scraps; the batter cracks.
There's pickled eggs in acid vats.
They'll never pass my lips!

We feast on grease and haddock that's
a thruppence ha'penny heart attack.
Every summer coming back
To Davy's Van-On-Sea.

Bridgnorth (Impressionist)

The Funicular purring;
its winding gear and bull heads
grind, chasing the heady scent
of lavender under hill

while warm rain-blots spatter
the rosemary and sweet pea
plants in the castle bailey,
releasing their clean, needle scents.

A summer cloudburst reveals
the colour trapped deep beneath
the monochrome veneer
of cobblestones. Rain shambles

across the cartway – gaining
speed as rock yields to asphalt
– and joins the Severn, slowing
down to skirt the low town.

Lullaby

The frenetic signal lost from Luxembourg
at 0045 hours nightly, gave me time
to retune the transistor to the long
wave, ghost whining of empty air.

White mono earphone crackling
as a warm and soothing treacle prayer
sounded; a languid, liquid lullaby
"Plymouth, Biscay, Finisterre..."

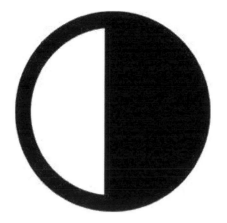

An Autopsy

i

Among mills, warehouses, tenements;
stone blackened; cars burned; metal rusted;
Each transformed by the neglect brought by

progress. Brittle breath clouds brittle glass,
as snow creaks underfoot. Reaching up
to break and enter an abandoned

Police Station. Apt audacity
from the sanctioned and disenfranchised.
There is shelter in this metaphor.

ii

Corridors of peeling paint. The stench
of rats and other vermin filling
lungs with a poisoned air of defeat.

Crawling through the wreckage of human
lives discarded; hypos; take outs; signs
that other victims of the decay,

abandoned this derelict building
in search of new life, or a final
willing journey to the underworld.

iii

Exhausted, guts ripped, heart torn, searching
for small comfort among the squalor;
a respite from perdition's sting;

he locates a clean room, cold and tiled,
a joyless aluminium table.
the faint odour of formaldehyde;

he rolls his coat to make a pillow
and sleeps on a mortuary slab.
The irony does not escape him.

Not Gold

A rucksack, mugger torn, spills a life
to the floor. Gathering the remnants;
wallet, money, destination gone;

no choice but a park bench; enamelled
metal and stale beer sticky; gooseflesh,
nipple hard, through skinny, ripped denim.

In Finsbury Park, he gains comfort
from constellations, bright as the light
in his naïve eyes. Orion sighs,

and pursues the Pleiades across
the Seven Sisters Road, losing them
below the Westway; calling him home.

Grímsbœ - Contains elements from 'The Orkneyinga Saga.'

We would take our gloves off
to see who could stand
the cold for longest.
Risking fingers to frostbite
as we broke the ice from the side
winders and trawled Iceland's shelf.

Long have we walked
in the mire...'

The last mooring came
without protest or payment
or warning. The town gutted
and filleted by gunship grey
and invertebrate wiles.

'...and made our way
through an abundance of shit.'

The ebb tide reaches
as far as the horizon
and different sails wave
against drear Spit skies.

'Elk-ships now trawl
from Grimsbœ...'

There was no Haven in the end.
No safe harbour for the latter
day invaders. An economic

repetition of the sacking
that transformed Óðinn's town.

'...across the Seagull's
Swamp to Bergen.'

The Fisherman's Wife

He climbs from the deck
past reeking holds,
the choke of ammonia
and week-old sweat
making him gack.

I see the skin on his palms
and fingers – torn and raw.
Capillaries broken,
in his fleshy cod cheeks,
from sub-arctic cold

and an over abundance
of rum. He sees the note
in hasty, thready ink
that condemns the town
and two thousand boats.

He shudders,
shoulders jumping,
and I know he wishes
he'd listened at school.

Stanlow

Every summer Sunday,
we walked the meadow,
collecting grasshoppers,
caterpillars and ladybirds

for no reason but to fill
Bryant and May match boxes
and forget. Cardboard insoles
disintegrating as we closed

in on the wetland marshes
to throw stones at godwits
and herons on the Mersey
sandbanks, laughing

as they hooped and boomed
before settling again
to feed on freshwater
shrimps. Then ships

brought a city
with no houses
and a tar sticky
heart. A promised

life of leather uppers
for the price of a smoke
sick river, acid in
the reign of oil;

a backdrop of pulp
fiction landscapes
and a name stolen from
a childhood idyll.

But the vitriol subsides
and shiv blade outlines
have softened with age
and ivy. Steel gantries

hold heat, creating thermals
for hawks to ride and prey
in the returned grassland.
Orchids bloom in undisturbed

pasture and hooping and
booming can be heard
once again.

The Road to Gentrification

Banksy's been
and sprayed the wall
with invective and wry
situationist drag

and pheromones
that attract the middle
classes who feel edgy
because they brunch

while Instagramming
their smashed avocado
and poached eggs on rye
to their kids in Thailand

who are on a gap year.

Cunts.

Laithe

The far barn was off limits;
a mantra drummed into us
from the day we moved in.
No access to be had beyond

the rotting stiles and snow
weathered paint that flaked
like falling sycamore keys
into black silage tea.

Slinking through the shadows
to dry rib doors with rust crackled
hinges and into charcoal gloom.
A steel arachnopolis of derelict

tractors and combineds resolves
as eyes adjust to a glut of dull
blades threatening to shiv,
as winter brittle sun bayonets

dust and gloam. Breath – misted –
wheezes from behind grey
stone wall and – curious – I pass
between web and trembling

shank to its forlorn source.
The stud bull, body crammed,
into a cell; too small. Job done,
abandoned until spring.

Head and horns stretch for
the elusive lambent shard,
brown eyes glaring. Gently
cooing, I reach to stroke his

brow. He starts and yawps, unused
to contact; confused by a moment
of caring. I knew better than
to open his pen and instead, turned

and pulled at the corrugated iron
holding the brittle laithe door together;
flooding his cell with sunshine
and fresh breeze. Eyes now closed,

he basks.

Uprooted

'You live in your bloody head far too much,'
said Dad, 'get into the world; away from
all those damned books and fancy. We're building
an orchard' – in the eastern paddock where
we had hand-raised the winter orphaned lambs;
mothers frozen, exhausted after

a hard labour in the top field. I had seen
forty-five saplings, their roots shivering
in the lazy Swale winds, lined up against
the Anderson; waiting for the cold kiss
of fresh dug loam. Petulant and without
the maternal warmth of the kitchen stove,

I stabbed at steeped turf with rusty auger,
making box string homes for stupid fucking
fruit trees. A bare smile passed as he saw pride –
unexpected – in my soil caked face. Arm
now slung round my shoulder, that brief look
hung like old telegraph wires; pregnant with

unseen information. Before the first shy
blossom showed, the farm had been sold
and developed. Box string starters
for identikit people, unmoved by wild
romances of unruly North Riding
orchards; the beacon that called me home

to bitter Allerton wapentake winters.

Hotel. Birmingham. 18.8.17. 06:15am

It's stifling, even with
the window open.
The bloody workmen
have woken me
with drills and diggers
with alarms that sound
like they will break
into 'Jingle Bells.'
Every few moments,
the threat of Christmas.

Half asleep in brown soupy
light I stare at a large picture
frame that shows a slender
body prone and elegant.
I study it for a moment
and marvel at the simplicity
of line before reaching
to wipe the sand
from my blear struck eyes.

The picture moves
and the mirror
reveals its treachery.

The mattress, too soft,
hides half of my body
in the depths of its
quicksand comfort,

conspiring with my longing
for a return to youth,
to show me the lithe
and elegant body I once had.
I allow myself a moment
of vanity then switch on
the light.

Hotel. Birmingham 19.8.17. 03:17am

Birmingham sleeps,
its illuminated
building works,
a shadow jungle
to trap the drunk
and wary.

Lost in the plastic
and sodium
labyrinth;
infernal circles
traced in brick
dust, he calls

"Kieran"
"Adam"
"Paul"

an inebriate incantation,
and no Lesser Key.

A tsunami of slurred
Anglo-Saxon oaths
issue and echo
as he drops
his polystyrene
tray of chips.

Surveying his loss
he walks away,

then turning to take
a run up he kicks
his chips into a wide
carbohydrate arc,

shouting "Rooooneeey"
and acting out
his World Cup
fantasies; escaping
his Inferno
on Paradise Circus.

Kiss Me Again Jack

So many years
since I felt the hoar
caress my cheek

with needle teeth.
Not breaking the skin
but bringing it to rude life . . .

Kiss me again, Jack.

Kevin

Kevin in the corner.
Quiet, out of place; never
quite comfortable in
the familial bosom.
And distant, like they knew.
'Too young to understand,'
they spat, hushed
and venom laced.

I remember the mustard
roll neck tops, Hai Karate
and porn star 'tache, receding
hair and twinkle in his eyes.
The understanding we had,
the unspoken camaraderie
we shared, the shock I felt
when he disappeared.

It took years to piece together
the barbs and puffing chests
at just the mention of his name,
and how the truth came
into pin sharp focus
when Uncle Paul chased
him through Daily Mail strewn
streets shouting something

about being seen
with another man.

The Goodfellow

This baleful repetition –
reaped and sown
by the click and the flash,
shackled in spider-murk
and animate tangle,

is no jest or gawde
but the felling of bodies;
a casual ruination.
This radiant, illuminate
magnesium blaze

nags a fallen Robin
naked to the foothills;
to the oak woods;
to the court
of the unSeelie.

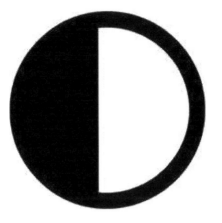

ABOUT THE AUTHOR

Will Vigar has an unhealthy obsession with Brutalist Architecture and revels in the beauty of lost causes. He writes poetry about land, sea and skewed nostalgia. He has edited collections of both poetry and comic books.

He is currently working on a collection of site specific poetry; a series of dérives exploring the cities and towns of Norway and a novel that is taking far too long to finish.

LUNAR TATTOOS is his first solo poetry endeavour.

Fiercely Northern, he lives in Hampshire and is not best pleased about it.

PREVIOUS PUBLICATIONS INCLUDE

As Author:
Going Home: Lost (Sold Out)
LIFE<infinite>DEATH (Sold Out)

As Contributing Editor:
Absent Ginsberg: An Anthology of Contemporary Poetry
Zombre: A Borderline Undead Anthology

He has also appeared in *The London Magazine* with an extract of the upcoming book 'Tales from the Urban Prairie,' a psycho-geographical study - in poetry and prose - of a now demolished, Brutalist Housing Estate in Sheffield.

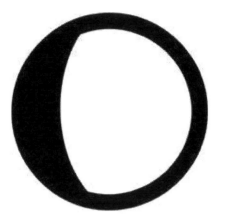

Printed in Great
Britain
by Amazon